# jason robert brown
# jason robe  ...own

**WITH A CD OF PIANO ACCOMPANIMENTS**
**PERFORMED BY JASON ROBERT BROWN**

# jason robert brown

ISBN 978-1-61780-644-5

**HAL•LEONARD®**
**CORPORATION**

7777 W. BLUEMOUND RD. P.O. BOX 13819 MILWAUKEE, WI 53213

In Australia Contact:
**Hal Leonard Australia Pty. Ltd.**
4 Lentara Court
Cheltenham, Victoria, 3192 Australia
Email: ausadmin@halleonard.com.au

Visit Hal Leonard Online at
**www.halleonard.com**

# thoughts from jrb

My favorite musical theater composers have all been formidable pianists: Leonard Bernstein, George Gershwin, Stephen Sondheim, Frank Loesser, Cy Coleman. When I was supposed to be learning Bach and Mozart for my piano lessons, I was instead spending countless hours playing through *West Side Story* and *Sunday in the Park with George*, relishing the challenge of reproducing the sounds I heard on the original cast albums and movie soundtracks. Meanwhile, I was writing songs inspired by my pop heroes: Billy Joel, Elton John, Carole King, Stevie Wonder – again, a group of pianists of great technical facility and truly individual style.

Over time, I developed a very specific personality of my own as a pianist, something that doesn't sound quite like anyone else. Of course, anything that is unique is going to be difficult to reproduce, and so it is with the notated piano parts of my songs. I work very hard to ensure that the written accompaniments really represent what I might play on any given day, and so there is a lot of detail – to some pianists, a daunting level of detail indeed. For twenty years now, I've had singers tell me that they can't find pianists who can play my songs "right." It's hard enough singing my material properly under the best of circumstances, but when the accompaniment isn't correct – when the singer doesn't feel supported by the pianist – it can make some of my stuff all but impossible to learn.

Hence these two volumes, which consist of eleven songs each for male and female voices (based on the gender for which they were originally written). The intention wasn't to provide performance tracks – I firmly believe that my songs, like all the best musical theater songs, depend on a give-and-take between singer and accompanist that can only be achieved live. Nor was the intention to document some "definitive" version of these accompaniments; I'm not sure I believe in such a thing. Simply put, these recordings are just one additional tool to help pianists and singers better understand and implement my intentions and style, to be used in conjunction with the published sheet music and the cast albums and solo recordings on which those songs have been featured.

Keen ears will note that what I am playing on these recordings is not always identical to the written accompaniments. It's not that I can't reproduce my music accurately (though there are sections of many of my songs that are beyond my technique); it's more that my songs continue evolving even after I publish the sheet music. For example, I've been playing "I'm Not Afraid of Anything" for over twenty years; it has in that time acquired all sorts of layers and colors that I didn't know about when I first wrote it down. Moreover (and more confusingly, as far as some pianists are concerned), an absolute fidelity to the notated score is not always the best way to represent my work – some of those insanely complicated licks and fills are really just descriptions of a gesture: a rhythm and a shape and an intention with possible notes attached. Sometimes the specific rhythmic "comping" in a song is open to variation, interpretation, even simplification. These recordings will help to clarify where the score is a fixed object and where it is more of a guide.

The best versions of any of my songs are the ones where the musicians (singers included) are deeply engaged with the emotions and the passions hiding underneath and around the written rhythms and pitches and lyrics. It is my hope that the recordings collected here help singers and pianists alike to bring these songs to life in their own way. Enjoy!

Jason Robert Brown
Los Angeles, California
January 2012

# contents

**Pianist on the CD:**
**Jason Robert Brown**

# biography

**JASON ROBERT BROWN** has been hailed as "one of Broadway's smartest and most sophisticated songwriters since Stephen Sondheim" (*Philadelphia Inquirer*), and his "extraordinary, jubilant theater music" (*Chicago Tribune*) has been heard all over the world, whether in one of the hundreds of productions of his musicals every year or in his own incendiary live performances. *The New York Times* refers to Jason as "a leading member of a new generation of composers who embody high hopes for the American musical." His four major musicals as composer and lyricist include: *13*, a musical written with Robert Horn and Dan Elish, which began its life in Los Angeles in 2007 and opened on Broadway in 2008; *The Last Five Years*, which was cited as one of *Time* magazine's 10 Best of 2001 and won Drama Desk Awards for Best Music and Best Lyrics; *Parade*, a musical written with Alfred Uhry and directed by Harold Prince, which premiered at Lincoln Center Theatre in 1998, and subsequently won both the Drama Desk and New York Drama Critics' Circle Awards for Best New Musical, as well as garnering Jason the Tony Award for Original Score; and *Songs for a New World*, a theatrical song cycle directed by Daisy Prince, which played Off-Broadway in 1995, and has since been seen in hundreds of productions around the world. *Parade* was also the subject of a major revival directed by Rob Ashford, first at London's Donmar Warehouse and then at the Mark Taper Forum in Los Angeles. In the wings: *Honeymoon In Vegas*, a musical adaptation of the 1992 film, written with Andrew Bergman; *The Bridges of Madison County*, a musical adapted with Marsha Norman from the bestselling novel; and a new chamber musical called *The Connector*. His orchestral adaptation of E.B. White's novel *The Trumpet of the Swan* premiered at the Kennedy Center with John Lithgow and the National Symphony Orchestra, and the CD was released on PS Classics. Jason is the winner of the 2002 Kleban Award for Outstanding Lyrics and the 1996 Gilman & Gonzalez-Falla Foundation Award for Musical Theatre. Jason's songs, including the cabaret standard "Stars and the Moon," have been performed and recorded by Audra McDonald, Betty Buckley, Karen Akers, Renée Fleming, Philip Quast, Jon Hendricks and many others, and his song "Someone to Fall Back On" was featured in the Walden Media film, *Bandslam*.

As a soloist or with his band The Caucasian Rhythm Kings, Jason has performed sold-out concerts around the world. His first solo album, *Wearing Someone Else's Clothes*, featuring his band The Caucasian Rhythm Kings, was named one of Amazon.com's best of 2005, and is available from Sh-K-Boom Records. His collaboration with singer Lauren Kennedy, *Songs of Jason Robert Brown*, is available on PS Classics. Jason's piano sonata, *Mr. Broadway* was commissioned and premiered by Anthony De Mare at Carnegie Hall. Jason is also the composer of the incidental music for David Lindsay-Abaire's *Kimberly Akimbo* and *Fuddy Meers*, Marsha Norman's *Last Dance*, David Marshall Grant's *Current Events*, Kenneth Lonergan's *The Waverly Gallery*, and the Irish Repertory Theater's production of *Long Day's Journey Into Night*, and he was a Tony Award nominee for his contributions to the score of *Urban Cowboy The Musical*. He has also contributed music to the hit Nickelodeon television series, *The Wonder Pets*. His scores are published by Hal Leonard. Jason currently teaches musical theater performance and composition at the University of Southern California.

For the new musical *Prince of Broadway*, a celebration of the career of Harold Prince, Jason will be serving as the musical supervisor and arranger. Other recent New York credits as conductor and arranger include *Urban Cowboy The Musical* on Broadway; Oliver Goldstick's play, *Dinah Was*, directed by David Petrarca, at the Gramercy Theatre and on national tour; and William Finn's *A New Brain*, directed by Graciela Daniele, at Lincoln Center Theatre. Jason was the musical director of the pop vocal group, The Tonics, with whom he performed at the 1992 tribute to Stephen Sondheim at Carnegie Hall (recorded by RCA Victor); he was the conductor and orchestrator of Yoko Ono's musical, *New York Rock*, at the WPA Theatre (on Capitol Records); and he orchestrated Andrew Lippa's *john and jen*, Off-Broadway at Lamb's Theatre (Varese Sarabande). In 1994, Jason was the conductor and arranger of Michael John LaChiusa's *The Petrified Prince*, directed by Harold Prince, at the Public Theatre. Additionally, Jason served as the orchestrator and arranger of Charles Strouse and Lee Adams's score for a proposed musical of *Star Wars*. Jason also took over as musical director for the Off-Broadway hit *When Pigs Fly*. Jason has conducted and created arrangements and orchestrations for Liza Minnelli, John Pizzarelli, Tovah Feldshuh, and Laurie Beechman, among many others.

Jason studied composition at the Eastman School of Music in Rochester, N.Y., with Samuel Adler, Christopher Rouse, and Joseph Schwantner. He lives with his wife and daughters in Los Angeles, California. Jason is a proud member of the Dramatist's Guild and the American Federation of Musicians Local 802 & 47. Visit him on the web at **www.jasonrobertbrown.com**.

# I'M NOT AFRAID OF ANYTHING

from *Songs for a New World*

Music and Lyrics by
Jason Robert Brown

**Moderate Folk Rock**

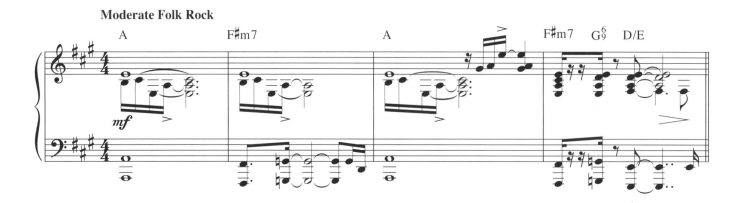

Jen-nie's a-fraid — of wa-ter, — I mean, she swims — so well, — but still, she's a-fraid of wa -

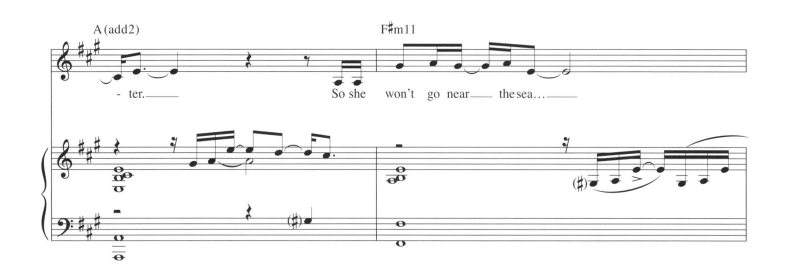

- ter. — So she won't go near — the sea…

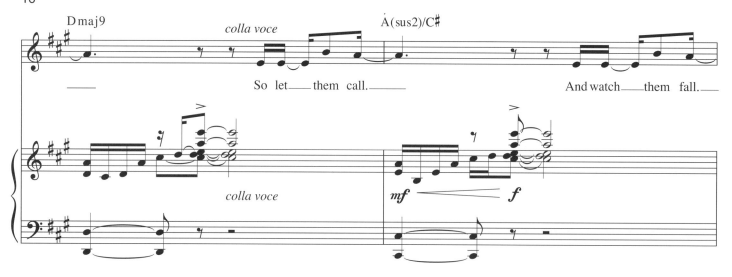

So let them call. And watch them fall.

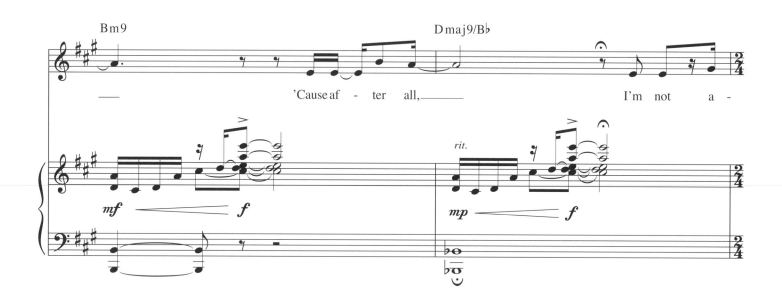

'Cause af - ter all, I'm not a -

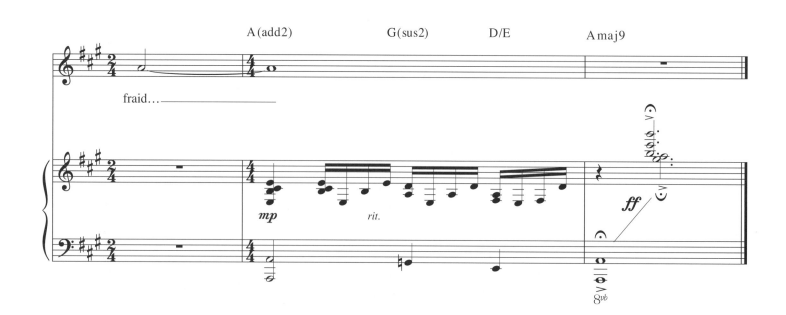

fraid...

# STARS AND THE MOON

## from *Songs for a New World*

Music and Lyrics by
Jason Robert Brown

**Folk Rock, gentle** (♩ = 60)

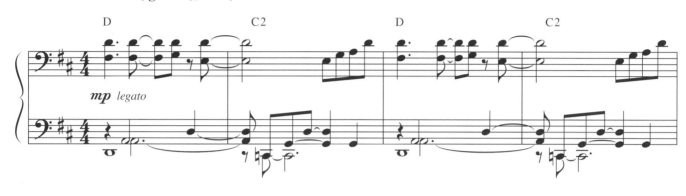

I met a man with-out a dol-lar to his name, who had no traits of an-y val - ue but his smile.

25

# CHRISTMAS LULLABY

from *Songs for a New World*

Music and Lyrics by
Jason Robert Brown

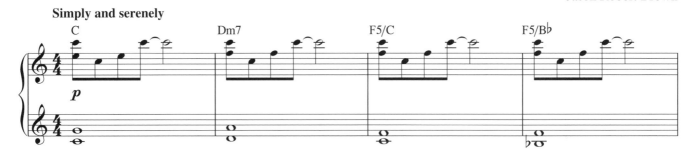

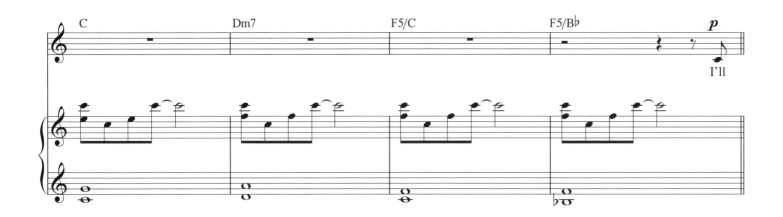

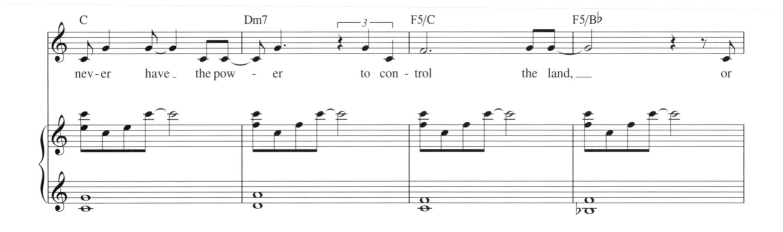

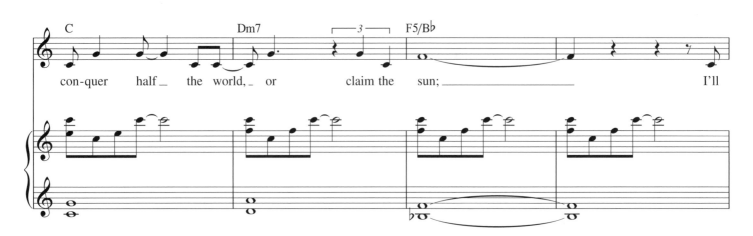

# STILL HURTING

## from *The Last Five Years*

Music and Lyrics by
Jason Robert Brown

Once the foun - da - tion's cracked    And

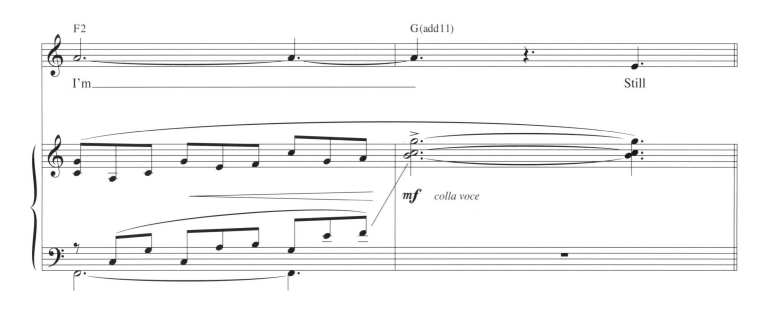

I'm _____    Still

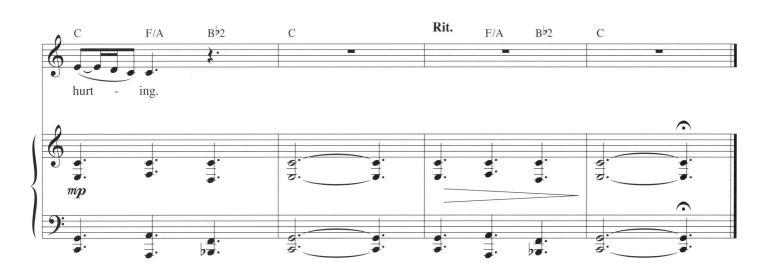

hurt - ing.

# A SUMMER IN OHIO

### from *The Last Five Years*

Music and Lyrics by
Jason Robert Brown

**Moderate shuffle** (♩=132-135)

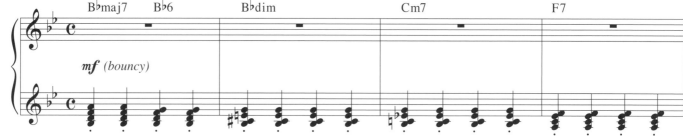

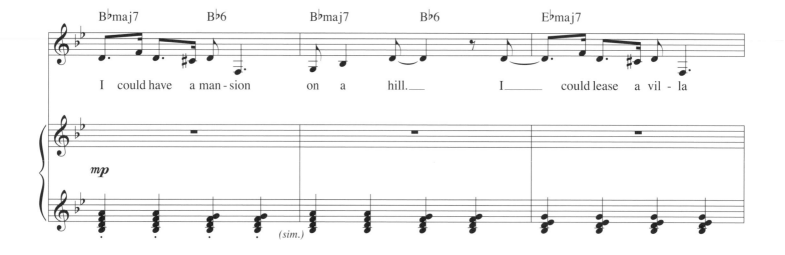

I could have a man-sion on a hill.__ I__ could lease a vil-la

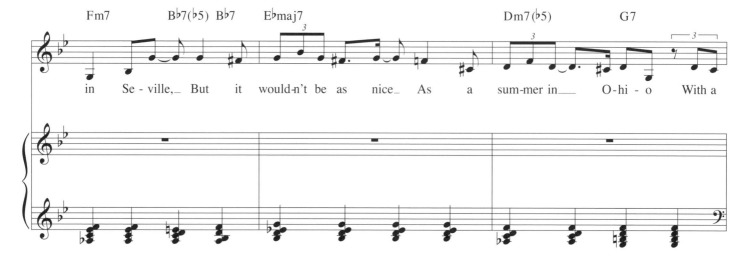

in Se-ville,__ But it would-n't be as nice__ As a sum-mer in__ O-hi-o With a

# I CAN DO BETTER THAN THAT

from *The Last Five Years*

Music and Lyrics by
Jason Robert Brown

# GOODBYE UNTIL TOMORROW

from *The Last Five Years*

Music and Lyrics by
Jason Robert Brown

# YOU DON'T KNOW THIS MAN

## from *Parade*

Music and Lyrics by
Jason Robert Brown

**Poco rubato throughout** (♩ = 116)

You don't know this man. You don't know a thing.

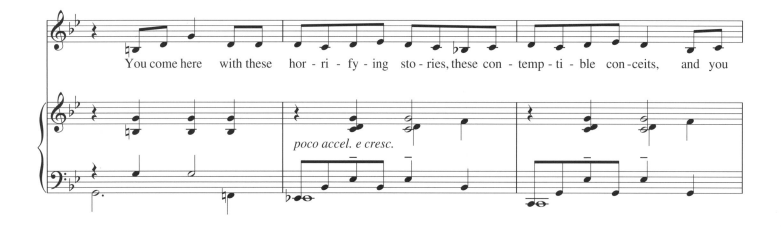

You come here with these hor-ri-fy-ing sto-ries, these con-temp-ti-ble con-ceits, and you

say you un-der-stand how a man's heart beats. And you don't know a thing.

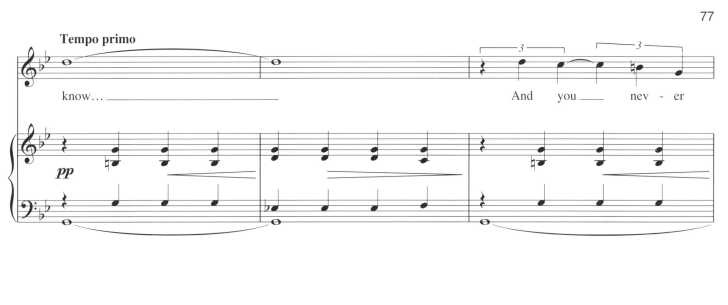

**Tempo primo**

know... And you nev - er

will. Not from me, not from an - y - one who knows him, not a

mor - sel, not a crumb, not a clue. I have

*poco rit.* **Freely** *pp*

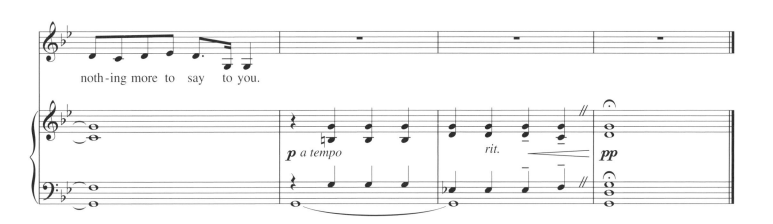

noth-ing more to say to you.

*p a tempo* *rit.* *pp*

# AND I WILL FOLLOW

## from the CD *Lauren Kennedy: Songs of Jason Robert Brown*

Music and Lyrics by
Jason Robert Brown

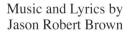

**Country Rock feel, with energy** (♩. = 72)

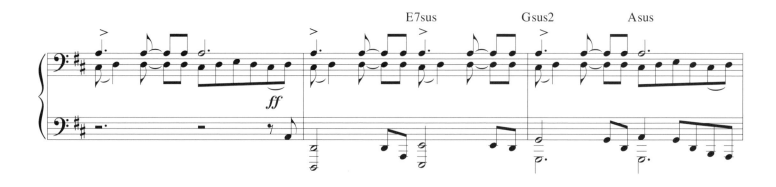

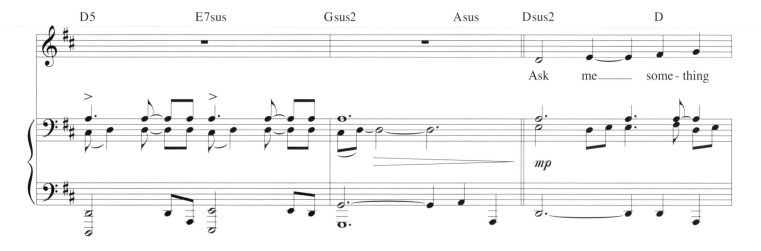

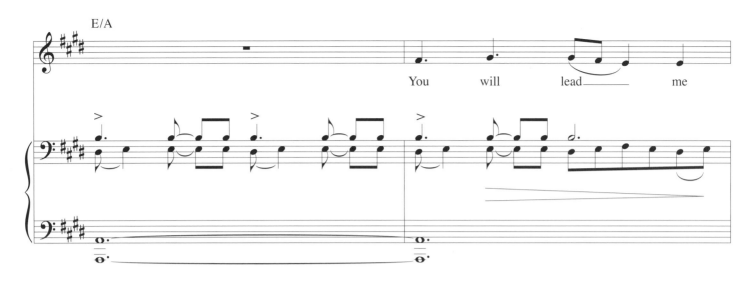

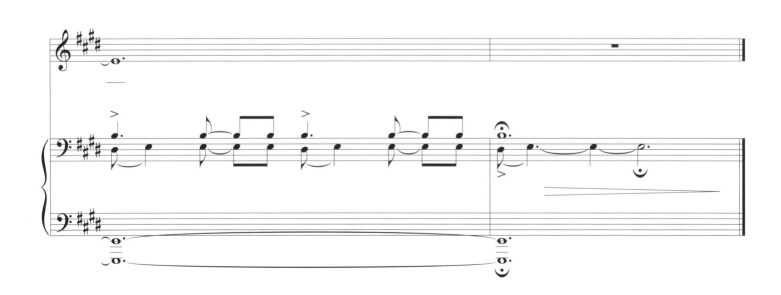

# MR. HOPALONG HEARTBREAK
from *Urban Cowboy The Musical*

Music and Lyrics by
Jason Robert Brown

**Bright Country Pop** (♩ = 132)

So__ long, Fare - well, Mis-ter Hop-a-long Heart - break,__ Thanks for the kicks, but I

guess we're through. Oh__ well, it's been fun hitch-in' up with a psy-cho like

# WHAT IT MEANS TO BE A FRIEND

from *13 The Musical*

Music and Lyrics by
Jason Robert Brown

# other **jason robert brown** vocal publications

| | |
|---|---|
| HL00313435 | **13 The Musical (Vocal Selections)** |
| HL00230091 | **In This Room — Vocal Duet and String Quartet (Score and Parts *plus* Piano/Vocal Duet version)** |
| HL00230089 | **Jason Robert Brown Plays Jason Robert Brown — Women's Edition, Book/CD** |
| HL00230090 | **Jason Robert Brown Plays Jason Robert Brown — Men's Edition, Book/CD** |
| HL00313304 | **The Jason Robert Brown Collection** |
| HL00313206 | **The Last Five Years (Vocal Selections)** |
| HL00313148 | **Parade (Vocal Selections)** |
| HL00313188 | **Songs for a New World (Vocal Selections)** |

# about the enhanced CD

In addition to piano accompaniments playable on both your CD player and computer, this enhanced CD also includes tempo and pitch adjustment software for computer use only. This software, known as the Amazing Slow Downer, was originally created for use in pop music to allow singers and players the freedom to independently adjust both tempo and pitch elements. Because we believe there may be valuable educational use for these features in classical and theatre music, we have included this software as a tool for both the teacher and student. For quick and easy installation instructions of this software please see below.

In recording a piano accompaniment we necessarily must choose one tempo. Our choice of tempo, phrasing, ritardandos, and dynamics is carefully considered. But by the nature of recording, it is only one choice. Similar to our choice of tempo, much thought and research has gone into our choice of key for each song.

However, we encourage you to explore your own interpretive ideas, which may differ from our recordings. This new software feature allows you to adjust the tempo up and down without affecting the pitch. Likewise, the Amazing Slow Downer allows you to shift pitch up and down without affecting the tempo. We recommend that these new tempo and pitch adjustment features be used with care and insight. Ideally, you will be using these recorded accompaniments and the Amazing Slow Downer for practice only.

The audio quality may be somewhat compromised when played through the Amazing Slow Downer. This compromise in quality will not be a factor in playing the CD audio track on a normal CD player or through another audio computer program.

## INSTALLATION FROM DOWNLOAD:

### For Windows (XP, Vista or 7):
1. Download and save the .zip file to your hard drive.
2. Extract the .zip file.
3. Open the "ASD Lite" folder.
4. Double-click "setup.exe" to run the installer and follow the on-screen instructions.

### For Macintosh (OSX 10.4 and up):
1. Download and save the .dmg file to your hard drive.
2. Double-click the .dmg file to mount the "ASD Lite" volume.
3. Double-click the "ASD Lite" volume to see its contents.
4. Drag the "ASD Lite" application into the Application folder.

## INSTALLATION FROM CD:

### For Windows (XP, Vista or 7):
1. Load the CD-ROM into your CD-ROM drive.
2. Open your CD-ROM drive. You should see a folder named "Amazing Slow Downer." If you only see a list of tracks, you are looking at the audio portion of the disk and most likely do not have a multi-session capable CD-ROM.
3. Open the "Amazing Slow Downer" folder.
4. Double-click "setup.exe" to install the software from the CD-ROM to your hard disk. Follow the on-screen instructions to complete installation.
5. Go to "Start," "Programs" and find the "Amazing Slow Downer Lite" application. Note: To guarantee access to the CD-ROM drive, the user should be logged in as the "Administrator."

### For Macintosh (OSX 10.4 or higher):
1. Load the CD-ROM into your CD-ROM drive.
2. Double-click on the data portion of the CD-ROM (which will have the Hal Leonard icon in red and be named as the book).
3. Open the "Amazing OSX" folder.
4. Double-click the "ASD Lite" application icon to run the software from the CD-ROM, or copy this file to your hard drive and run it from there.

## MINIMUM SOFTWARE REQUIREMENTS:

### For Windows (XP, Vista or 7):
Pentium Processor: Windows XP, Vista, or 7; 8 MB Application RAM; 8x Multi-Session CD-ROM drive

### For Macintosh (OSX 10.4 or higher):
Power Macintosh or Intel Processor; Mac OSX 10.4 or higher; MB Application RAM; 8x Multi-Session CD-ROM drive